Jesus Teaches Me
BELIEVING

Jesus Teaches Me BELIEVING

The Boy Who Gave His Lunch Away
He Remembered to Say Thank You
The Seeds That Grew to Be a Hundred

An ARCH BOOKS Gift Collection

*An Inspirational Press Book
for Children*

First Inspirational Press edition published in 1998.

Inspirational Press
A division of BBS Publishing Corporation
386 Park Avenue South
New York, NY 10016

Inspirational Press is a registered trademark of BBS Publishing Corporation.

Published by arrangement with Arch® Books, a division of Concordia
Publishing House, 3558 S. Jefferson Avenue, St. Louis, Missouri 63118-3968.

Library of Congress Catalog Card Number: 98-72389

ISBN: 0-88486-212-7

Printed in Mexico.

The Boy Who Gave His Lunch Away

JOHN 6:1-15 FOR CHILDREN

Written by
Dave Hill

Illustrated by
Betty Wind

Joel lived a happy life
down by Lake Galilee.
"We have a farm," he liked to say,
"for Mom and Dad and me."

His dad grew barley, oats, and wheat
for baking rolls and bread.
"What we don't eat we give away,"
was what he always said.

Joel knew what Father meant,
for EVERYONE needs bread.
"But why are some folks poor," he asked,
"when we are so well fed?"

"It isn't fair at all, I know,
but someday," Father said,
"the good Messiah will be here,
and He will be our King.
Then there will be no rich or poor.
We'll all have everything!"

So Joel helped his folks at work.
He rose each day at four
and washed the pots and scrubbed the pans
and swept and mopped the floor.
He helped his dad fill up the bags
of bread to give the poor.

One warm June day a neighbor stopped
to buy a loaf of bread.
"I'm on my way to see the King.
He's right nearby," he said.

"A king?" said Joel.
"Right nearby?
You must be fooling me!"
The stranger shook his head.
"I'm not!
Why, people say that He
is God's Messiah – here at last!
Why don't you come and see?"

"Is this the man named Jesus, sir?"
asked Father with a smile.
"Because, if so, my son can go
and see Him for a while."

"The very man!" the neighbor cried.
"You've heard of Him, I see!"

"I've heard He's kind and loves the Lord.
That's good enough for me!"

"You'd better take this lunch along, my boy," his mother said. "I've packed you up two fish and five small loaves of barley bread."

"I won't need that!"
cried Joel. "Why,
the King will
feed the poor!"

But Father told him, "Take it, son,"
as they went out the door.

So up the road, with lunch in hand,
the two went with a smile.
They soon came to a noisy crowd
stretched out for half a mile.
"He must be near! We'll see the King
in just a little while!"

"That's Jesus there!"
a voice called out,
and Joel turned to see.
There stood a man
as plain and poor
as any man could be!

He ran up close
where he could see,
and hear what Jesus said.
"Is this the King –
this plain, poor man?
I'm glad I brought
some bread!"

Then Jesus spoke; His voice was strong:
"Bring all the sick to Me!"
And Joel stared as lame folks walked
and blind men cried: "I see!"

As Joel watched, he saw the sick
made whole and well and strong.
"Our King! Our King!" a shout rose up
from all who came along.

Then Jesus turned
and raised a hand
and spoke out
loud and clear:
"The kingdom tha
God promised you
you see
already here!

"The kingdom
the Messiah brings
is full of
love and joy.
It's like a happy
dinner that
a king gives
for his boy."

The day grew short, and someone cried:
"I wish we had some bread!"
A man beside the Teacher spoke:
"How will these folks be fed?"

When Joel heard, he ran right up:
"I have some bread and fish.
I'll gladly share them with the crowd
if that is what you wish!"

"Five loaves? Two fish? For all this mob?"
asked one man with a frown.
But Jesus took the food and said,
"Have everyone sit down."

"We thank you, Father," Jesus prayed
and blessed and broke the bread.
Then His disciples passed it out
till ALL THE CROWD was fed.

"A miracle!" somebody cried.
"There's food for all to share!"
The helpers even gathered up
twelve baskets full to spare.

"Hooray! Hooray!" the people cheered.
"Shall we crown Jesus king?
He'll always give us what we need,
and we'll have everything!"
But Jesus turned and hurried off.
He wanted no such thing!

DEAR PARENTS:

Like Joel, people in New Testament times looked for the promised Messiah to come and establish His kingdom. In their deep longing they hoped for a time when the hungry would have enough to eat and the poor would have all their needs supplied.

In Jesus, the Messiah, the kingdom of God came according to promise. Jesus announced the Kingdom in words: "The time is fulfilled, and the kingdom of God is at hand" (Mark 1:15). He performed many signs to indicate the coming of God's kingdom, or gracious rule, over men. The feeding of the 5,000 with five loaves and two fishes is such a sign. This feeding miracle reminds us of parables in which Jesus compared the kingdom of God to a great dinner banquet. He invites all people, good and bad, rich and poor. God provides for the needs of people in generous abundance at this banquet. There is plenty for all, even when our faith is too small to see how God can provide. Resources at the banquet may be limited, but Christ uses them to feed the thousands who come to Him.

The people who were fed by the loaves and fishes were impressed by Jesus' powers. They wanted to make Him a bread king to satisfy their hunger and other needs of daily life. Because they misunderstood the King and His kingdom, "Jesus withdrew again to the hills by Himself" (John 6:15). He is more than a supplier of free bread. He is the "Bread of Life" (John 6:35), who brings the rule of God to us and gives us His goodness and love.

Will you help your child see the meaning of our story as the work of Christ putting God's kingdom into action? Will you help him experience the joy and abundance of life in Christ's church?

THE EDITOR

HE REMEMBERED TO SAY THANK YOU

Luke 17:11-19 FOR CHILDREN

Written by Victor Mann

Illustrated by Betty Wind

In a little town on the top of a hill,
At the end of a narrow street,
A kind old priest with tears in his eyes
Wiped the dust from his tired feet.

He sat with Hiram and stared at the ground.
The words were hard to say.
"Hiram," he said, "I have very sad news.
You must leave this town right away.

"You have a disease called leprosy.
I wish it were not true.
But you must go so your family and friends
Don't get the sickness from you.

"No one should ever come close to you.
So if you should meet a stranger,
Cry out very loudly, 'Unclean! Stay away!'
To warn him about the danger."

Hiram left town. He felt hurt and alone
When everyone called him "unclean."
He wanted to say good-bye to his friends,
But they were afraid to be seen.

They hid behind stairways, peeked around
  doors,
And climbed up the tallest trees.
They were so frightened they stayed far away
From their friend with the dreaded disease.

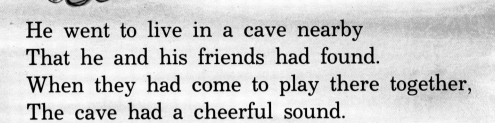

He went to live in a cave nearby
That he and his friends had found.
When they had come to play there together,
The cave had a cheerful sound.

He leaned against a sycamore tree
And looked at the clear blue sky.
He wanted to dance and sing again.
Instead he started to cry.

Tears trickled down his thin, pale cheeks
As he prayed, "God, let me be free.
I'll thank You and serve You every day
If you'll cure my leprosy."

For many years Hiram lived alone.
Then very late one night
Nine more lepers came with such wonderful news
It made Hiram dance with delight.

"Jesus is coming this way tomorrow.
We've come to see Him," they said.
"He must have the power to heal leprosy.
He brought people back from the dead."

Hiram kept dancing and
shouting for joy.
His happiness spilled
everywhere.

Jesus was coming
the very next day.
God had answered
his prayer.

He tossed and turned in his bed all night.
He was much too excited to rest.
What would he say when Jesus came?
Would Jesus hear his request?

Long before the sun came up,
When the air was very still,
He got up quickly and left the cave
And climbed to the top of the hill.

He waited and watched the road for hours.
His body began to ache.
He closed his eyes and nodded his head.
He couldn't stay awake.

The sun was low in the orange sky
When Hiram awoke with a start.
He jumped to his feet and looked around.
Fear filled his pounding heart.

"I missed Him," Hiram cried to himself.
"Something always goes wrong.
How could I miss my chance to be healed?
Why did I sleep so long?"

Then far away he heard the sound
Of a noisy, laughing crowd.
He saw the dust from their tramping feet
Rise in a swirling cloud.

He rubbed his eyes and shook his head
To be sure it wasn't a dream.
A happy cheer got stuck in his throat
Then escaped in a squeaky scream.

The lepers all ran down the hill.
"We're tired of being alone.
Jesus, Master, have mercy on us.
Please heal us so we can go home."

A hush fell over the startled crowd.
Fear danced in their terrified eyes.
They began to shout, "Keep away from us."
But Jesus silenced their cries.

He turned to the men, who were still far away,
And called out across the field,
"Go into the village and find the priest
To show him that you have been healed."

The countryside rang with happy shouts
As the ten men rushed to the priest.
They couldn't wait to be welcomed home
With a party, or maybe a feast.

But suddenly Hiram stopped and remembered
The promise he made in his prayers.

He ran back and said, "I thank you, Lord,
For showing me how much God cares."

Jesus was silent, then asked the crowd,
"Where are the other men?
Why has only one man returned
When God's gift was given to ten?"

"Of all those men only this one remembered
To thank God for what he received.
Go home to your friends," Jesus said to Hiram.
"You are well because you believed."

DEAR PARENTS:

Hiram the leper is the perfect image of each of us as sinner. Hiram was isolated from his community and forced to see himself as not-OK. Have your child point out to you how ugly and lonely leprosy made Hiram feel, e. g., people hid from him, shouted at him, he cried, etc.

Be sure to explain, however, that having any disease — including leprosy — is in no way a mark of being sinful. Disease is a result of sin in the world, but not a punishment for an individual person's sins — Jesus' miracles of healing show us how happy and whole God wants all of us to be.

Just as Hiram's leprosy separates him from other people, so his healing comes with a crowd, first the other lepers, then Jesus and his followers. Christianity always means people. Jesus makes Hiram and the other lepers OK by having them go back to their community — to their priest. And the healed lepers expect to have a party to celebrate their return.

The result of being made to feel really OK by Jesus is Hiram's ability to say thank you. When we know we are OK through Jesus, we acknowledge our need for help and can help others. We open up. Hiram was doubly healed: He looked better and he felt better.

Let your child describe his/her own feelings of not being OK and subsequent feelings of ugliness and loneliness. Then help him/her realize Jesus' OK that permits us to love and affirm others. A kiss and hug would be an appropriate way to conclude.

THE EDITOR

the seeds that Grew to Be a hundred

Matthew 13:1-17 FOR CHILDREN

Written by Victor Mann   Illustrated by Don Kueker

Hundreds of people pressed close to Jesus
While He sat by the lake one day.
They had gathered around from every town
To hear what He would say.

They crowded so close He could hardly move.
"A boat is what I need."
So He sat in a boat and told them a tale
Of a farmer planting seed.

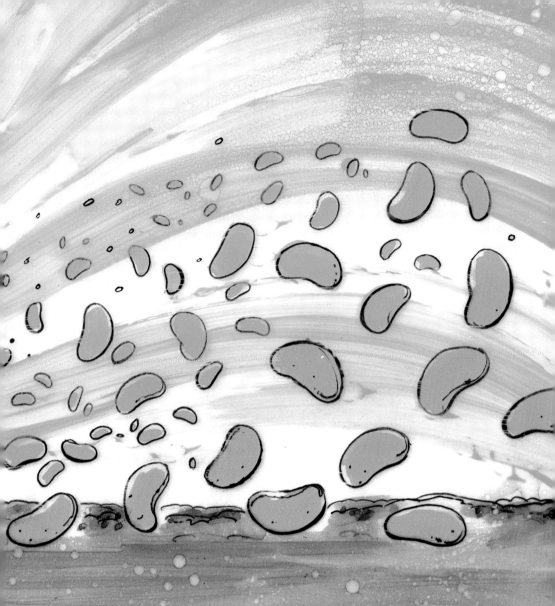

A farmer was scattering seeds in his field.
They flew with a whispering sound.
All of them wanted to grow to be healthy.
But some fell on hard, packed ground.

Landing! Bouncing! Rolling! They stopped.
What a terrible place to fall!
At the edge of a path where everyone walked,
How could they ever grow tall?

"Let us in! Let us in! Please let us in!"
The seeds began to cry.
"Our food and water is underground.
If we stay up here we'll die."

People walked by and trampled the seeds,
Crushed them under their feet.
The seeds called loudly, "Help us, please!"
While the birds settled down to eat.

But the hard, packed ground refused to hear,
And the people walked merrily on.
Trampled by feet and eaten by birds,
Soon every seed was gone.

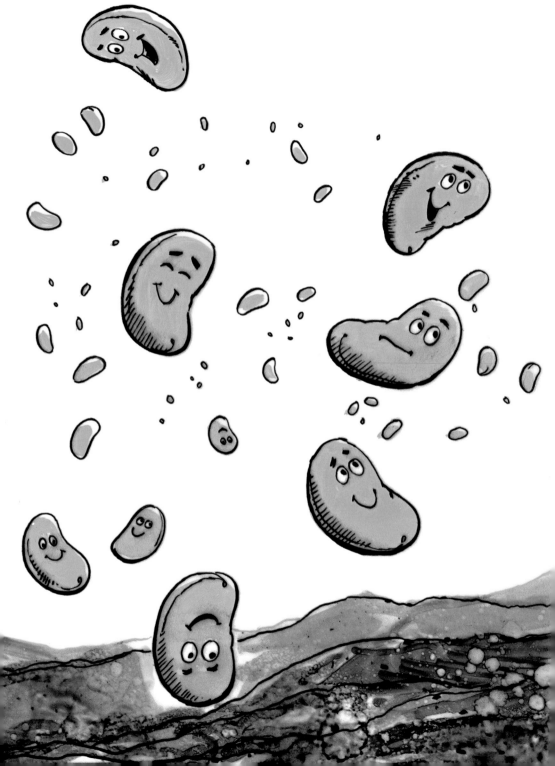

The morning air was speckled with seeds
That flew with a whispering sound.
They wanted to grow to be healthy plants.
But they fell on rocky ground.

It was warm in the soft, thin layer of earth
That covered the cold, hard rock.
And the seeds felt safe because they fell
Where people didn't walk.

Soon tiny pinpoints of green pushed up.
Leaves spread to catch the light.
The roots underground ran out to get food.
Some went left, some down, and some right.

But they ran into rock below shallow earth.
"Move aside. We need to find water."
They wiggled and pushed to get by the rocks.
The ground became dry, the sun hotter.

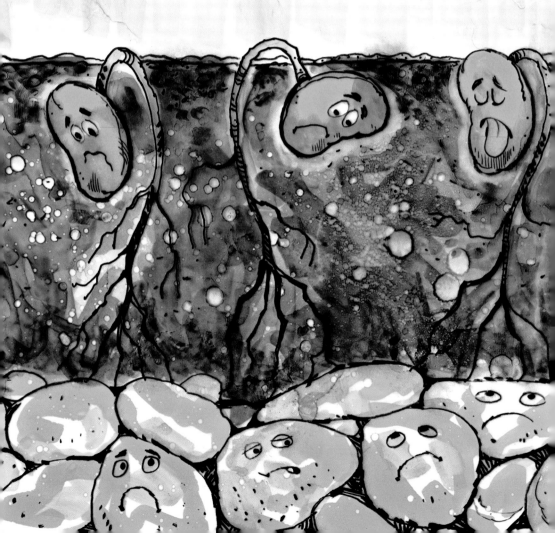

But the rocks didn't care about the plants.
"Remember! We were here first."
Without enough water the plants became weak.
Their heads bowed. They died of thirst.

The farmer walked in every direction.
The air was filled with seeds.
They wanted to grow to be healthy and strong.
But the ground was filled with weeds.

Good seeds and weeds grew up side by side.
The weeds and thorns grew fast.
At first they shared food, water, and sun.
But their friendship didn't last.

The weeds grew tall, took over the land.
The thorns grew to be much stronger.
They crowded the plants and blocked the sun.
The plants could take it no longer.

"Move over! Don't crowd! Give us light!
We need more room to grow."
"Harumph! Too bad," said the wicked thorns.
"We're bigger than you are, you know.

"Fight if you like, but we will win."
The laughing thorns sneered with pride.
Fight they did, but the thorns were strong.
The plants grew weak, choked, and died.

The farmer walked on, scattering seeds.
They grew as well as they could.
And some of them did grow tall and strong,
For some of the ground was good.

Asleep in the warm, wet earth they waited
Until it was time to start growing.
Soon out of the earth and into the sunlight
Tiny green sprouts began showing.

Slowly they stretched toward the sky,
Sent deep roots that never got tired
Of gathering food to make the plant grow.
The earth gave them all they desired.

Soon at the top of thin, straight bodies,
Tall, golden heads formed and grew.
Each of those heads had a hundred seeds.
One had a hundred and two.

"We don't understand why you told that story,"
The disciples said when He was done.
"It's our job to preach about God, not farming.
Your story must just be for fun."

"God's Word is like the seeds," said Jesus.
"It goes everywhere to be heard.
But it grows in people, not in the ground,
If their ears will just hear His Word.

"Wherever it grows it causes people to love
Because God loves us all so much.
We learn to love people all over the world,
Most of them too far to touch.

"Now, some people listen, but others don't.
So the meaning of the story is clear.
Don't be like ground where seeds can't grow.
Open your ears and hear."

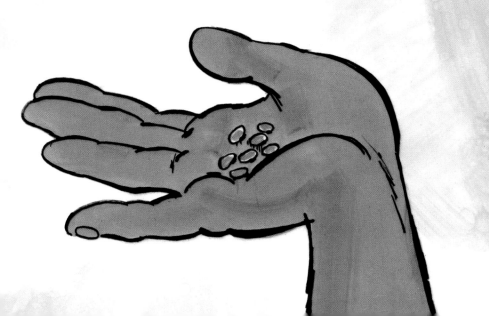

DEAR PARENTS:

The seeds that fell on hard, packed ground were trampled by passersby and eaten by birds. These are the people who hear God's Word but let it go in one ear and out the other. Satan has so hardened their hearts that the seed cannot put down any roots at all.

The seeds that fall on rocky ground put out tentative roots but soon die for lack of moisture. These are the people who hear God's Word and make a tentative commitment. But as soon as their newly adopted faith puts them in an uncomfortable or painful situation, their commitment withers and dies.

The seeds choked out by weeds and thorns: these are the people who hear God's Word and commit themselves to it. But they have a lot of other commitments too—success, wealth, power, etc. And after a messy battle, these other commitments win out.

The seeds in good soil are what every sower hopes for. They are the kind of people every Christian aspires to be; theirs is the kind of Christianity every Christian hopes to lead others to.

Join your children in praying that God will help the seed sink deep roots and flourish in your own hearts and in the hearts of all that hear.

THE EDITOR